AVOCA
Soups

Contents

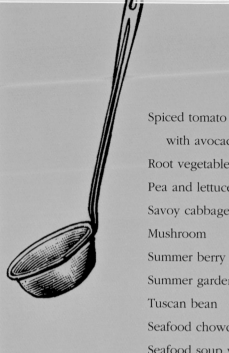

Introduction

oups at Avoca are pretty central to what we do. At least two are made from scratch in each of the cafés every day. Sometimes more, it rather depends on how many customers come through the door. In winter we tend to cook more robust soups, these range from thick and creamy vegetable soups through to what are really meals in bowls (spiced beans and sausages spring to mind). In summer our soups tend to be lighter: broth based and vibrant in colour, like pea, or summer minestrone.

A soup is rather wonderful: often humble ingredients cooked together for half an hour or so. We tend to keep ours vegetarian, something that happens in a lot of restaurants, but there is no need to stick rigidly to this. You can get all fancy with a soup, but we prefer to concentrate on delivering big bold flavours. That way you get satisfaction of the best kind, which is rather important to us.

A soup can become quite substantial. Even with a hunk of bread it can become a serious lunch. Favourites include pea soup and a bacon sandwich, spinach soup and chicken salad, or watercress soup and a hunk of blue cheese and bread. There are endless variations and ways to tweak soup (of which more later). You can swirl in relishes, add toasted seeds, top with flavoured oils and butters, and even add additional chopped vegetables, like the Spanish do with gazpacho. There are no end of garnishes too, among them fried chorizo, crumbled grilled Parma ham, or croûtons.

Soups come in many ways, most of them pretty healthy. You can eat a soup warm or cold, smooth or chunky. Some work rather better one way than another, but there is every reason to account for personal preference – if you like a smooth soup left chunky then why not?

Thick soups are probably our most popular, but then there are quick ones, slow ones, meat-based ones, vegetable ones and fish ones. The list really is almost endless and that is before you have got on to the big ones - chowders and minestrones, gumbos and stews. For at some point a soup can become a stew. Some frequently do. Perfect for mid-week suppers, or as starters for dinner parties, starters that are easy to prepare ahead.

Most soups demand a good stock, something to give body and depth to the whole assembly. A good stock is not diffiult to make and we have lots of short-cuts to show you (see page 70).

All recipes feed four unless otherwise stated.

Carrot and ginger

*2 onions, peeled and
chopped
30g butter
2 large potatoes, peeled
and chopped
6 carrots, peeled and
chopped
3cm piece fresh root ginger,
peeled and finely chopped
1 litre vegetable or
chicken stock*

*This is a simple to make and healthy soup. The addition of
ginger giving it an unexpected dimension*

Gently sauté the onion in the butter for 15 minutes without
colouring. Add the potato and carrot and toss until well
coated. Add the ginger, season with salt and pepper and
pour in the stock. Bring to the boil, lower the heat and
simmer for 20 minutes, or until the vegetables are tender.

Blitz, check seasoning and serve.
Crème fraiche makes a good garnish.

Variations

Carrot and coriander
*Before seving stir in two tablespoons of roughly chopped
coriander leaves*

Carrot and orange
*Add the juice and finely grated zest of an orange at the end
This is a particular favourite of children.*

Carrot and parsnip
Use equal quantities of each.

Broccoli, toasted almonds and Greek yoghurt

150g blanched slivered almonds
50g butter
2 tablespoons vegetable oil
1 onion, peeled and chopped
2 potatoes, peeled and chopped
1 litre light chicken stock
250g broccoli, stems and florets, cut nice and small (the stems, particularly, as they can be tough)
4 dessertspoons full-fat Greek-style yoghurt

At Avoca we use a lot of seeds, nuts and herbs to add an extra dimension. Almonds and broccoli are great partners, one seems to spark the other off to good effect.

Spread the almonds out on a roasting tray and toast under the grill for a minute or two until golden. You need to toss them a little during this time so they colour evenly. Transfer to a plate and allow to cool.

Soften the butter in the oil and gently cook the onion without browning for 10 minutes. Add the potatoes, season with salt and pepper, then pour in the chicken stock. Bring to the boil and simmer for 15 minutes, or until the potatoes are cooked, adding the broccoli and two thirds of the almonds 5 minutes before the end. Then purée the soup.

Check the seasoning and reheat in a clean pan. Ladle into bowls, add a dollop of yoghurt, scatter over the reserved almonds and serve. (You can only add the yoghurt after the soup has been heated or it splits.)

Add

a

dollop

of

yoghurt

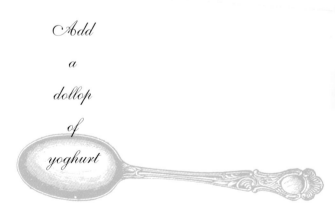

Classic French onion

25g butter
olive oil
500g white onions, peeled
and sliced
½ teaspoon picked thyme
leaves
125ml dry white wine
1 litre beef stock
½ French stick
75g Gruyère cheese, grated

This is one of those all-time greats that no innovation can improve on. We make this with beef stock but you can use vegetable stock if you prefer. The quality of the stock here is important though.

Heat the butter and 2 tablespoons of oil in a saucepan and add the onion. Cook over the lowest heat for 20 minutes, or until softened. Add a seasoning of salt and pepper and continue to cook for 40 minutes, stirring frequently. The onions will slowly take on a golden colour. You need to cook them to a mahogany brown, so they are well caramelised.

Add the thyme and white wine and cook off most of the liquid. Add the stock. Bring up to simmering point, cover and simmer for 20 minutes, stirring occasionally.

Slice the bread, one round per bowl, and drizzle with olive oil. Grill until brown and crispy. Ladle the soup into bowls and place the grilled bread on top. Generously sprinkle with the cheese and place under a preheated grill for 1 minute, or until brown and bubbling.

Summer bean minestrone

Serves 6-8

3 tablespoons olive oil
2 onions, peeled and diced
2 potatoes, peeled and diced
1.25 litres vegetable stock
300g courgettes, trimmed
and chopped
250ml full-fat milk
100g French beans, cut into
3cm lengths
100g podded and shelled
broad beans
100g frozen peas
1 tablespoon chopped mint
leaves
2 handfuls baby spinach
1 dessertspoon roughly
chopped mint leaves
4 teaspoons crème fraîche

This is what would be known as a primavera or spring soup in Italy. It makes use of the vegetables that are abundant at the time.

Heat the oil and gently sauté the onion over a low heat for at least 10 minutes until softened. Add the potatoes and continue to cook for 10 minutes, stirring occasionally. Add the stock, bring to the boil and simmer for 10-15 minutes. Add the courgettes and cook for 5 minutes. Remove from the heat, add the milk and blitz in a blender

Add the French beans, simmer for 2 minutes, then add the broad beans, and simmer for 1 minute. Add the frozen peas, and season with salt and pepper. Bring almost to the boil, then remove from the heat.

Add the mint and spinach, check seasoning, stir through and serve with a teaspoon of crème fraiche for each serving

Variations

Replace the courgettes with a similar weight of asparagus.
Replace the spinach with a similar amount of rocket.

Heat the oil and gently sauté the onion

'I live

on

good

soup,

not

on

fine

words.'

Moliere

'Soup puts the heart at ease,

calms down the violence of hunger,

eliminates the tension of the day,

and awakens and refines the appetite.'

Auguste Escoffier

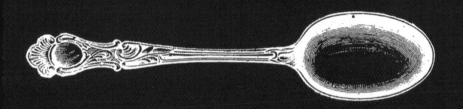

'Beautiful soup! Who cares for fish, game

or any other dish? Who would not give all else

for two pennyworth of beautiful soup?'

Lewis Carroll, Alice in Wonderland

Spiced Moroccan chickpea, marinated lamb and gremolata

2 racks of lamb, cut into
12 cutlets
2 lemons
1 bunch coriander
1 garlic clove, peeled and
finely chopped
1 teaspoon nigella seeds
1/2 teaspoon turmeric
a pinch of chilli powder
olive oil

Spiced chickpeas

onion, peeled and chopped
2 carrots, peeled and finely
diced
2 butternut squash, peeled,
seeded and cut into 3cm
cubes
celery stalk, trimmed and
finely chopped
1 x 400g can chickpeas,
rinsed
and drained
2 garlic cloves, peeled and
finely chopped
3cm piece fresh root ginger,
peeled and grated
1 teaspoon cumin seeds
teaspoon ground coriander
1/2 cinnamon stick
1/2 teaspoon tomato purée
1 litre light chicken stock
1 tablespoon gremolata
(see page 19)

This is something of a meal in a bowl. The gremolata, a simple combination of garlic, parsley and lemon zest, brings a real brightness to this substantial soup. Gremolata also works well over grilled meat or fish.

Put the lamb cutlets into a dish. Zest the lemons and reserve. Squeeze the juice into a bowl and add the finely chopped stems from the coriander, along with the next four ingredients. Add the lamb cutlets, season everything with salt and pepper and toss well. Set aside.

Heat 2 tablespoons olive oil in a pan and gently sauté the onion without colouring for 10 minutes. Add the carrot, butternut squash and celery and continue cooking without colouring for a further 10 minutes. Add the chickpeas, garlic, ginger, cumin, coriander, cinnamon and tomato purée and coat well in the oil. Add the chicken stock and bring to the boil. Turn the heat down and simmer for 20 minutes.

Brush the coriander marinade off the lamb, lightly oil, season with salt and pepper and fry or grill for 4-5 minutes on each side or until cooked. Serve the lamb on top of the spiced vegetables and chickpeas and sprinkle on the gremolata

Variation

You can use the same marinade, doubled in quantity, with a butterflied leg of lamb which will feed rather more than the two racks above

Seared salmon and noodle

4x 100g skinless salmon fillets
soy sauce
2 tablespoons saké
2 garlic cloves, peeled and minced
3cm piece fresh root ginger, peeled and grated
1 tablespoon runny honey
150g somen noodles
vegetable oil
1 chilli, finely chopped
2 carrots, peeled and finely sliced
2 leeks, trimmed and finely sliced
1 stick lemongrass, tough outer leaves removed
1 litre fish or light chicken stock
4 heads pak-choi or Asian greens, or 150g sprouting broccoli, roughly chopped
1 bunch coriander, roughly chopped
2 limes, halved

This is a broth-based Oriental style soup. For all our enthusiasm for vegetable-based thick soups a bit of change is always welcome.

Put the salmon in a dish. Combine 1 tablespoon of the soy sauce, the saké, garlic, ginger and honey. Pour over the salmon, toss gently so the salmon is well coated, cover and set aside for an hour.

Cook the noodles according to the instructions on the packet, drain and refresh under cold water.

Heat 2 tablespoons of oil in a hot wok and stir-fry the chilli, carrot and leek for 2 minutes. Smash the lemongrass and add to the wok along with the stock. Bring to the boil and simmer for 5 minutes or until the vegetables are just cooked.

Heat the grill, brush the salmon with oil, season lightly with salt and grill on both sides for 5 minutes or until cooked.

Add the noodles to the hot broth in four bowls along with the pak-choi. Serve with the salmon on top. Scatter over the coriander and serve with soy sauce and limes to season.

Variations

Instead of the salmon, you could use prawns grilled with chilli and garlic, or char-grilled chicken breast, similarly marinated and combined with mushrooms.

Celery and
Cashel Blue cheese

50g butter
nion, peeled and chopped
3 potatoes, peeled and
roughly chopped
1 litre light chicken stock
1 head celery, trimmed
and chopped
g Cashel Blue cheese, plus
a little extra to garnish
100ml double cream
4 teaspoons crème fraîche
1 tablespoon finely
chopped parsley
1 tablespoon finely
chopped chives

A luxurious start to a dinner party or an almost complete supper when paired with a glass of red wine.

Melt the butter and add the onion. Cook over a gentle heat without colouring for 10 minutes. Add the potato and stock, season with salt and pepper and cook for a further 20 minutes. Add the celery 10 minutes before the end.

Purée the soup, adding the cheese and double cream as you do. Gently reheat in a clean pan. Check the seasoning and serve with the crème fraîche, crumbled remaining cheese and the herbs.

Tip

Cashel Blue is one of Ireland's best artisan cheeses, however other blue cheeses can be substituted. Try to choose something crumbly rather than creamy.

Curried parsnip and apple

2 onions, peeled and chopped
50g butter
1 heaped teaspoon curry powder
2 potatoes, peeled and chopped
1 large Bramley apple, peeled, cored and chopped
6 parsnips, peeled and chopped
1 litre vegetable stock
4 teaspoons double cream or crème fraîche

Apple and parsnip is one of those combinations that seems such an obvious one once you've tasted it. The parsnip's sweetness is perfectly complemented by the apple's tartness. Something for those colder autumn or winter days.

Gently sauté the onion in the butter for 10 minutes witho colouring. Add the curry powder and cook for a further 2 minutes, stirring to prevent it catching. Add the potato, apple and parsnip, and stir to coat everything evenly. Add the stock and simmer over a low heat, partially covered, f 20 minutes, or until the vegetables are cooked. Blitz and a the cream.

If you want a more pronounced apple flavour you can ad glass of apple juice (125ml).

Apple crisps

These make a nice addition if you are serving this soup fo dinner party, for example.

Core an eating apple and slice thinly. Sprinkle the discs w icing sugar and place on greaseproof paper on a baking sh Bake in a very low oven, 110C/gas mark ¼ for 2 hours, c until dried. Cool completely on a wire rack.
These will keep for a few days in an airtight container.
To garnish put a teaspoon of crème fraiche on the soup a lay an apple crisp or two against it.

Making your own curry powder

1 teaspoon ground coriander
half teaspoon turmeric
half teaspoon ground cumin
1 teaspoon sweet paprika

Combine all the ingredients and proceed

Butternut squash and gremolata

1 butternut squash
2 celery stalks
3 leeks
2 carrots
30g butter
1 teaspoon black mustard seeds
600ml light chicken stock

4 slices bread, crusts removed and cut into squares
4 tablespoons olive oil

Gremolata
1 tablespoon finely chopped parsley
2 garlic cloves, peeled and finely chopped
finely grated zest of 1 lemon

This soup can be made with any squash or pumpkin but in our experience butternut squash is by far the most successful, and the most reliable of the squash family to buy.

Peel, trim and chop the vegetables. Combine in a casserole with the butter and colour over a gentle heat for 10 minutes. Add the mustard seeds, a seasoning of salt and pepper and continue cooking for 3 more minutes. Add the chicken stock, cover and simmer for 20 minutes, or until the vegetables are just soft. Check seasoning, cool and liquidise.

Gently sauté the bread in the olive oil until golden brown, then drain on kitchen paper.

Combine the parsley, garlic and lemon zest to make gremolata. Serve the soup with the croûtons and a sprinkling of the gremolata.

Variations

A herb butter, or garlic or chilli-infused slick of olive oil works really well with this soup.

Salsa verde

1 tablespoon finely chopped parsely
1 tablespoon capers, rinsed and roughly chopped
2 tablespoons finely chopped gherkins
1 teaspoon Dijon mustard
1 garlic clove, peeled, finely chopped and mashed with a little salt
2 tablespoons olive oil

Combine all the ingredients in a bowl and check seasoning. Spoon on to the soup just before serving

Cauliflower cheese

1 large onion, peeled and
finely diced
1 large baking potato, peeled
and diced
50g butter
1.2 litres vegetable stock
1 large cauliflower, divided
into small florets
110g mature Cheddar
cheese, grated
300ml pint full-cream milk
4 teaspoons double cream
1 dessertspoon chopped
fresh chives

Cauliflower cheese is something of a comfort dish. Easy, simple and reassuring. This recipe simply turns it into a soup.

Gently sauté the onion and potato in the butter over a very lc heat for 10 minutes, stirring occasionally, until the onion is translucent. Add the stock and cauliflower and season with salt and pepper. Bring to the boil, reduce the heat and simm for 15 minutes, until the vegetables are cooked through. Purée in a blender, then return the soup to the pan and bri back to the boil. Remove from the heat and stir in the chee and milk. Reheat gently, adjust the seasoning and serve topped with a spoonful of cream and some chopped chive

Convenience

 soup can take as little as 15 minutes to prepare. From start to finish. A soup made from tinned pulses, for example, will still taste fantastic when combined with fresh garlic, some herbs and stock. Far better than something coming out of a packet. White bean, garlic and rosemary for example, or lentil and spiced butter.

Even a vegetable soup, courgette and herb say, or mushroom really can be prepared in 20 minutes. How much more convenient can you get?

ou can make a sou into a meal if it has enough going on in i As we point out elsewhere, a soup can easily become a stew. Which means supp

But a soup can also team up with oth things. Sandwiches spring to mind, or salads. Together they make quite a feast. sort of ying and yang thing. Try a pea sou with bacon rolls, or a tomato soup with roast chicken sandwiches, the latter spike with a little chlli perhaps.

We often think of soup as a lunchtime thing, but soup works well in the evening too. By itself or before other things.

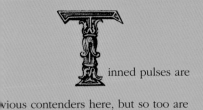

inned pulses are
vious contenders here, but so too are
ngs like tinned sweetcorn, frozen peas
d spinach and tinned tomatoes. Vegetables
a also make fine soup. Savoy cabbage
th cream and crispy bacon for example,

We tend to think of soups in terms of
getables or meat or fish, but there are
cellent soups like the Italian *stracciatella*
essence eggs, Parmesan and parsley
oked in stock. You can make a fine and

similar soup with peas in place of the parsley.

Cold meats gently poached in stock, think
chicken and beef particularly, make great
soups. Sprinkled with cheese or containing
a poached egg they become feasts.

Storecupboard &
creative soups

Courgette and almond

50g butter
1 onion, peeled and chopped
1 potato, peeled and chopped
600ml vegetable stock, chilled
3 courgettes, finely chopped
25g ground almonds
125ml double cream, plus extra to serve
125ml milk
Flaked almonds, to serve

Melt the butter in a large pan, add the onion and potato and cook over a very low heat for 5 minutes. Add the stock, bring to the boil, then reduce the heat and simmer for 20 minutes or until the potato is cooked. Add the courgettes, bring back to the boil and simmer for 5 minutes. As soon as the courgettes are cooked, remove the pan from the heat and stir in the almonds, cream and milk. Purée in a blender then reheat gently and season to taste. Serve topped with a few toasted flaked almonds and a swirl of cream.

And a swirl of cream. And a swirl of cream. And a swirl of cream.

Celeriac and toasted hazelnut

100g shelled hazelnuts
50g butter
onion, peeled and chopped
2 potatoes, peeled and chopped
1 celeriac, peeled and cut into 5cm cubes
1 litre chicken stock
1 teaspoon picked thyme leaves
100ml whipping cream

Celeriac is a root vegetable, with lots of stringy bits attached. Not, perhaps, the most attractive of vegetables. What you get however, is a rich creamy celery flavour. This is no time for a peeler. Chop away with a sharp knife.

Heat a dry frying pan over a moderate heat and toast the hazelnuts. You need to move them round a bit so they get coloured all over. Transfer to a plate and allow to cool. Roughly chop.

Melt the butter over a low heat and add the onion. Sauté gently without colouring, for 10 minutes. Add the potato and celeriac, season and cook for 2 minutes. Add the stock and thyme and bring to the boil. Lower the heat and simmer for 15 minutes or until the celeriac is tender.

Add two-thirds of the hazelnuts, and purée the soup.

Return to a clean pan and reheat, stirring in the cream. Serve with a scattering of the remaining chopped hazelnuts.

....

Variation

red peppers, roasted, peeled and deseeded (you can use ones from a jar which should already be peeled)
small handful of sun dried tomatoes, soaked in warm water (or straight from the jar if they are in oil)
2 garlic cloves, peeled and finely chopped
2 tablespoons chopped flat parsley
200ml red wine vinegar
70g toasted flaked almonds
half of teaspoon sweet paprika
generous dash of Tabasco
450ml extra virgin olive oil

Romesco sauce
This sauce adds both punch and bite and is useful as a garnish for other soups.

Combine all the ingredients apart from the olive oil in a processor. Switch on and drizzle in the olive oil to form a thick paste the consistency of cream. This will keep for several days in the fridge.

Chilled cucumber and mint

2 cucumbers
300ml plain yoghurt
1 garlic clove, peeled, sliced
and mashed with a little salt
600ml light chicken or
vegetable stock
1 bunch mint, leaves
roughly chopped
200ml single cream

Peel, seed and grate the cucumbers. Place in a colander and toss with a teaspoon of salt. Leave to drain for 15 minutes.

Combine the yoghurt, garlic and stock and stir in the mint. Rinse the cucumber and squeeze gently. Add to the yoghurt and stock. Stir in the cream and refrigerate. When ready to serve, check seasoning, and pour into iced bowls.

Thai chicken noodle

100g medium egg noodles
1 litre chicken stock
2 Kaffir lime leaves
1 stick lemongrass, outer
leaves removed and finely
chopped
3cm piece fresh root ginger,
peeled and finely chopped
2 tablespoons fish sauce
(nam pla)
juice and finely grated zest
of 2 limes
2 chicken breasts, finely
sliced
2 heads pak-choi,
roughly chopped
150ml coconut milk
1 red chilli, or to taste,
finely sliced
coriander leaves to serve

The aim in Thai cooking is to end up with something light, refreshing and invigorating. Too often a heavy hand with the coconut milk results in something overly creamy. A light hand and lots of tasting is recommended.

Cook the noodles according to the instructions on the packet. Refresh in cold water and drain.

Combine the stock, lime leaves, lemongrass, ginger, fish sauce, lime juice and zest in a saucepan, and bring to the boil. Add the chicken, pak-choi and coconut milk, and simmer for 2 minutes or until the chicken is cooked.

Add the noodles, heat through and serve, sprinkled with chilli and coriander

Variations

Coconut milk is very rich and fattening. It is perfectly possible to leave it out and you will still have an authentically flavoured Thai soup. Or you could substitute with soya milk. You can also add beansprouts, spring onions or garden peas 2 minutes before the end of cooking. Or carrot batons, which will need about 10 minutes' cooking in the soup.

Petit pois and mint

onion, peeled and chopped
1 medium potato, peeled
and chopped
50g butter
1.2 litres vegetable stock
350g petits pois
A bunch of mint, finely
chopped
300ml pint milk

If your garden runs to fresh peas, then pick and eat with pleasure. Most of us, however, use frozen, and peas are the one vegetable that most chefs would rather use frozen. The sugar in a pea starts to convert to starch as soon as it is picked, giving it a woody flavour – far better the sweetness of a frozen pea.

Sweat the onion and potato in the butter over a very low heat for 10 minutes, without colouring. Add the stock, bring to the boil, then cover and simmer for 20 minutes or until the potato is tender. Raise the heat, stir in the peas and simmer for 2 minutes. Remove from the heat, add the mint and then immediately purée in a blender, adding the cold milk as you do so. Season with salt and pepper, reheat gently and serve.

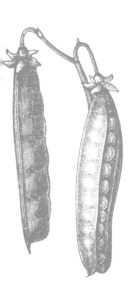
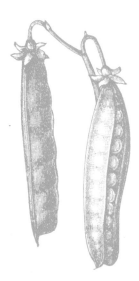
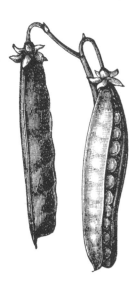

Asparagus with crème fraîche and smoked salmon

500g asparagus stalks
50g butter
1 onion, peeled and finely chopped
2 medium potatoes, peeled and roughly chopped
800ml chicken stock
50ml double cream
150ml crème fraîche
100g smoked salmon, roughly torn into strips

An indulgent soup undoubtedly, but in early summer when asparagus is at its best this is a perfect soup to start a feast.

Trim and discard any really tough parts of the asparagus stalks. Cut four of the asparagus tips off, thinly slice them lengthways, and set them aside for the garnish. Chop the remaining asparagus into 3cm lengths.

Melt the butter in a saucepan and add the onion. Soften for 5 minutes, stirring occasionally. Add the potato and continue to cook for a further 5 minutes. Keep the heat low, you don't want the onion to colour at all. Add the chicken stock, bring up to simmering point, season with salt and cook, uncovered, for 20 minutes. Add the asparagus 5 minutes before the end. Blitz immediately, along with the cream.

To serve, reheat gently stirring in the crème fraîche towards the end. Distribute between 4 bowls, lay the smoked salmon on top and top with the reserved sliced asparagus tips

Garnishes

A garnish always adds
a little extra:

Herb or spiced butter.

Flavoured oil (maybe with
chilli).

Toasted nuts – almonds
and hazelnuts are Avoca
favourites.

Freshly chopped herbs –
parsley, tarragon, chives,
basil are all popular.

Yoghurt adds freshness and
zing (but will curdle if
reheated or it gets too hot).

Sauces or salsas add zip:

rouille on toast
(traditionally used in the
fish soups of Provence, see
page 57)

Romesco sauce (a heady

Sauces
and salsas

combination of chilli,
tomatoes, garlic and nuts
from Spain, see page 25)

tomato relish (one is given
on page 60)

pistou/pesto (which you
can make yourself but
there are some excellent
jars to buy

salsa verde (herbs, capers
and olive oil)

gremolata (a simple but
very effective combination
of parsley, lemon zest and
garlic, see page 19)

Serving

An elegant way to serve
soup is to place prepared
vegetables or other
garnishes in soup bowls
the table and then bring
the soup in a tureen so
people can pour their ow
soup on top. For example
you could use croûtons
and peas for a pea soup,
or cooked asparagus tips
with asparagus soup.

Crispy bacon goes with
quite a few soups.

lded to soup, bread

courages the idea of a

al. You might rub toast

th garlic and then douse

with olive oil; simply

ve chunks of bread with

l-fashioned butter; or go

e whole hog and fry off

me croûtons.

Croûtons can be cubed

ead or slices of baguette.

her toss in oil and toast

the top of a hot oven

0°C/gas mark 4) or cook

a frying pan.

Parmesan toasts, sliced

guette sprinkled with

eese and grilled, add a

ole extra dimension to

oup.

Potatoes

If you are making a

smooth soup a potato

added to the other

ingredients lends

everything a welcome

creaminess, something

smooth without being rich.

To call it a vegetable cream

would be unfair, but it

gives you the general idea.

Anybody making soup is

likely to end up freezing at

least some of it. By far the

best way to do this is in

polythene bags. Do write

the date and name of the

soup on the bag, as you

won't remember. Don't

throw several bags into the

freezer together, as they will

stick like glue. Stocks can

be frozen in the same way.

Need your frozen soup or

stock in a hurry? Place the

bag in a large bowl of cold

water for 10 minutes. The

contents should then slip

out relatively easily into a

saucepan and can be

reheated with the lid on

from frozen.

Low GI minestrone

2 onions, peeled
and chopped
olive oil
2 carrots, peeled and diced
1 red and 1 yellow pepper,
seeded and diced
1 chilli, finely chopped
4 garlic cloves, peeled and
finely chopped
a handful of pearl barley,
rinsed in several changes
of water
2 celery stalks, diced
1 litre light chicken stock
1 x 400g can tomatoes
1 teaspoon tomato purée
1 x 400g can chickpeas,
rinsed and drained
2 sprigs oregano, finely
chopped
1 teaspoon picked thyme
leaves

The GI refers to the glycemic index. This measures the speed at which foods are broken down by the body to form glucose the body's source of energy. High GI foods break down quickly and leave you feeling hungry. Low GI foods break down more slowly and leave you feeling fuller, longer. It is these low GI foods that form the core of the diet.

Gently sauté the onion in 4 tablespoons olive oil for 10 minutes. Add the carrots, peppers, chilli, garlic and barley. Toss in the oil and cook for 2-3 minutes. Add the celery, stock, tomatoes and tomato purée and cook for a further 15 minutes, or until the vegetables are just cooked. Add the chickpeas and cook for a further 5 minutes.

Add the fresh herbs, check the seasoning and serve.

Variations

You can add char-grilled chicken breasts, grilled sausages or chorizo to turn this into a more substantial supper dish.

Serve with a dollop of crème fraîche and a scant 1/2 teaspoon harissa per serving for something of a chilli kick

Semi-sun-dried tomato pesto along with extra herbs give a robust, fragrant finish

Tomato and roasted pepper

1 onion, peeled and
chopped
4 tablespoons olive oil
1 garlic clove, peeled
and finely chopped
750ml pints vegetable or
chicken stock
400g can of tomatoes
A sprig of thyme
1 teaspoon tomato purée
pinch of ground cinnamon
2 red peppers, roasted
(see page 68) and roughly
chopped
About 1 teaspoon lime juice

The secret of this recipe is the roasting of the peppers. This brings out their natural sweetness which gives this soup its extra depth of flavour.

Sauté the onion in the olive oil for about 10 minutes, until translucent. Add the garlic and cook for 1 minute. Then add the stock, tomatoes, thyme, tomato purée, cinnamon and some salt and pepper. Bring to the boil, reduce the heat and simmer for 20 minutes.

Stir in the roasted peppers and then purée the soup in a blender. Reheat gently, add the lime juice to taste and check the seasoning.

Chickpea, goat's cheese and gremolata

1 onion, peeled and finely chopped
olive oil
1 x 400g can chickpeas, rinsed and drained
1 chilli, finely chopped
750ml light chicken stock
1 x 400g can tomatoes
4 slices goat's cheese, roughly crumbled
1 tablespoon gremolata (see page 19)

At Avoca we cook all our pulses from scratch. Which means soaking and a lot of boiling. When cooking for smaller numbers however, tinned chickpeas, particularly some of the brands found in delicatessens – are a good use of sensible convenience foods

Soften the onion in 4 tablespoons olive oil for 10-15 minutes without colouring. Add the chickpeas and chilli, coat well with oil, and then add the chicken stock. Bring to the boil and cook for 15 minutes over a low heat. Add the tomatoes 5 minutes before the end of cooking. Season with salt and pepper. Allow to cool for 10 minutes and liquidise. Bring back to the boil.

To serve, ladle the soup into bowls, spinkle over the goat's cheese and then the gremolata.

Variation

Pinch of dried chilli or harissa

½ teaspoon of ground cumin

Drizzle with chilli oil to serve

Tomato and roasted fennel

*2 heads fennel, trimmed,
cored and sliced
olive oil
onion, peeled and chopped
2 garlic cloves, peeled and
chopped
2 x 400g cans tomatoes
1 teaspoon tomato purée
500ml vegetable stock
1 teaspoon pastis (optional)
4 teaspoons crème fraîche
a few sprigs of chervil*

*This is a very popular soup, one of those perfect partnerships
that seem so obvious, once you've tried it. Roasting the fennel
renders it soft and almost creamy.*

Preheat the oven to 190C/gas mark 5. Place the fennel in a
roasting tray, drizzle with 4 tablespoons olive oil and season
with salt. Place at the top of the oven and roast for 30-40
minutes or until well coloured and tender.

Gently sauté the onion in a saucepan in 4 tablespoons
olive oil for 15-20 minutes without colouring. Add the garlic,
cook for 1 minute and then add the tomatoes, tomato purée
and stock. Season with salt and pepper and cook for 15
minutes.

Add the roasted fennel to the tomato along with a splash
of pastis, if using, and blitz to a purée.

Check the seasoning, heat through and serve with a
dollop of crème fraiche and a sprig of chervil.

check the seasoning

Watercress

3 generous bunches
watercress
50g butter
2 medium onions, peeled
and finely sliced
2 medium potatoes, peeled
and diced
1 large garlic clove, peeled
and crushed
1 litre vegetable or light
chicken stock
a pinch of freshly grated
nutmeg
2 tablespoons thick cream or
crème fraîche

An old-fashioned classic perhaps, but one that is impossible to better. Make sure your watercress is vibrant and fresh, anything below par will disappoint.

Pick over the watercress and wash, discarding any really tough stalks, and roughly chop. Melt the butter in a large pan and sweat the onion for 10 minutes without colouring. Add the potato and garlic and cook for a further 5 minutes. Add the stock, season with salt and pepper, bring to the boil and simmer for 20 minutes.

Add the watercress and cook for a scant 5 minutes or until the watercress stalks are tender. Season with nutmeg.

Liquidise, stir in the cream or crème fraîche and check the seasoning. You can serve either hot or cold. If reheating take care not to let the soup boil.

Spiced bean and sausage

2 onions, peeled and
chopped
olive oil
2 carrots, peeled and sliced
2 celery stalks, diced
2 red peppers, cored, seeded
and diced
1 chilli, finely chopped
4 garlic cloves, peeled and
finely chopped
1 bay leaf
1 teaspoon finely chopped
rosemary
1 litre light chicken stock
1 x 400g can tomatoes
1 teaspoon tomato purée
1 x 400g can kidney beans,
rinsed and drained
8 large spicy sausages

Quite a substantial soup to say the least. Not something that you'd need to partner with anything much more, except perhaps a green salad.

Gently sauté the onion in 4 tablespoons olive oil for 10 minutes. Add the carrot, celery, peppers, chilli, garlic, bay leaf and rosemary. Toss in the oil and cook for 2-3 minutes. Add the stock, tomatoes and tomato purée and cook for a further 15 minutes, or until the vegetables are just cooked.

Add the kidney beans and cook for a further 5 minutes. Check the seasoning.

Meanwhile, lightly oil the sausages and grill until golden, about 10 minutes, turning two or three times. Slice and add to the soup and simmer for 5 minutes. Check the seasoning and serve.

Variations

Serve with a spoon of pesto on top, or with a handful of rocket leaves.

If you add some penne at the same time as the stock, this becomes a substantial supper dish. You may, in this case, need to cook everything for a few more minutes to get the pasta tender.

How thick can you get?

thin soup – unless it's a consomme – tends to lack body and bite. Here are a few ways to thicken.

Cook the soup, uncovered, for 30 minutes over a low heat. The evaporation will both thicken and concentrate the flavour. The snag is colour loss, so if you are preparing a green vegetable soup hold back on adding the green vegetable until you've done your reducing.

Add a potato, roughly chopped, along with the other vegetables at the start. This is the preferred route at Avoca, a natural way to thicken and enrich.

At Avoca we only use flour in mushroom soup and chowder, see pag 48 and page 55. It is important to coo the flour out, at least 5 minutes, more like 10, otherwise your soup is likely to taste of flour.

The Avoca soup mantra

equipment

It's easy to get all hi-gh about equipment. To be honest, most of what is contained in any well-equipped kitchen will be sufficient for making soup: chopping board, sharp knife, a good large saucepan (especially for stock).

There is however a gadget that is essential to soup making. You need to be able to blend, blitz, or whiz the ingredients in a thick soup. For this you will need a blender or mouli legume. The latter has the advantage of going in the dishwasher but more importantly, purees the ingredients at a low temperature.

Start with the freshest and best-quality vegetables. Cook for the shortest time possible, as you want your soup to taste fresh, not stewed.

Any green vegetables should be added as close as possible to the end of cooking. They should barely cook and then be blitzed immediately so that they hold their flavour and colour.

Spiced tomato and kidney bean with avocado relish

1 onion peeled and chopped
1 red pepper, cored and chopped
olive oil
2 garlic cloves, peeled and crushed
¼ teaspoon ground cumin
¼ teaspoon ground coriander
pinch cayenne
¼ teaspoon paprika
½ teaspoon dried oregano
1 400g tinned tomatoes
1 tablespoon tomato puree
½ 400g tin red kidney beans drained and rinsed
300ml vegetables stock
juice 1 lime

4 slices French bread
1 garlic clove, halved
1 tablespoon grated Parmesan

The influence is South American and Spanish, the result is more meal in a bowl than soup. Robust, hearty and warming.

Gently saute the onion and red pepper in 2 tablespoons olive oil for 10-15 minutes, or until soft and lightly coloure. Add the garlic, spices and herbs and salt and pepper to taste. Cook for a further 2 minutes, stirring continuously so the spices lose their raw aroma and smell sweet and rounded.

Add the tomatoes and the pureé, drained kidney beans and stock and simmer for 20 minutes. Check the pepper an onion is soft, allow to cool for 5 minutes and liquidise. Stir in lime juice to taste and gently reheat, checking seasoning.

Brush the bread slices with a little olive oil, rub with th cut side of garlic and grill on one side until golden brown. Turn over and sprinkle over Parmesan, put under the grill briefly.

Spoon the soup into bowls, top with the avocado relishand the French bread.

Avocado relish

1 avocado, destoned, peeled and roughly chopped
juice of 1 lime or lemon
half teaspoon finely chopped red chilli or to taste
1 tablespoon finely diced red onion
pinch ground cumin
pinch ground coriander
1 tablespoon chopped fresh coriander

Combine all the ingredients and season.

Root vegetable

onion, peeled and chopped
50g butter
2 potatoes, peeled and chopped
4 carrots, peeled and chopped
2 celery stalks, chopped
leeks, washed and chopped
1 parsnip, peeled and chopped
1 litre vegetable stock
4 teaspoons double cream or crème fraîche
tablespoon chopped parsley

Simple, and all the better for that. Serve in mugs for ease and accessibility, children seem to like the informality.

Cook the onion in the butter for 10 minutes without colouring. Add the potato, carrot, celery and leek, and sauté gently for 5 minutes. Add the parsnip and continue cooking for a further 5 minutes, seasoning with salt and pepper.

Add the stock, bring to the boil and simmer for 20 minutes or until the vegetables are soft. Allow to cool slightly and purée in a blender.

Reheat, checking seasoning as you go, and serve with the cream and parsley.

Pea and lettuce

1 litre vegetable stock or light chicken stock
400g peas in their pods (or frozen petits pois)
50g butter
2 heads little gem lettuce, cores cut out and leaves shredded
150ml crème fraîche
1 bunch chervil or mint

A strange idea? Wait till you try it. You'll be surprised how much flavour lettuce can have.

Bring the stock to the boil. Remove the peas from their pod and place the pods in the boiling stock. Remove from the heat and leave for 10 minutes. Liquidise and push through fine sieve, discarding the pulp. If using frozen peas, skip th stage.

Melt the butter in a saucepan and add the peas and lettuce. Cover with a lid and cook over a moderate heat fo 5 minutes. Add the warm stock to the peas and lettuce and season with salt and pepper. Liquidise, return to the pan, check seasoning and reheat slowly.

Remove from the heat, stir in the crème fraiche and sprinkle over the chervil

. . . .

Variation
Garnish with crumbled feta and slices of dry-fried Parma ham.

Savoy cabbage and chestnut

50g butter
onion, peeled and chopped
500g Savoy cabbage, cored
and roughly chopped
1 bunch parsley, finely
chopped
12 peeled chestnuts
available in jars or vacuum
packed), roughly chopped
freshly grated nutmeg
1 litre light chicken stock
100ml double cream

Something of a seasonal treat come the autumn. There is something very comforting in the sweet mealiness of chestnuts when combined with the king of cabbages.

Melt the butter over a moderate heat and sauté the onion until softened but not coloured, about 10 minutes. Add the cabbage, parsley and chestnuts and season with nutmeg (about a quarter), salt and pepper. Cover and sweat down for about 20 minutes, turning occasionally.

Add the stock, bring to the boil and simmer for 10 minutes, or until the cabbage is tender. Stir in the cream, check the seasoning and serve.

check the seasoning

Mushroom

25g butter
2 onions, peeled and very finely chopped
1kg mixed mushrooms, finely chopped
75g plain flour
1 litre vegetable stock
600ml full-cream milk
1 teaspoon chopped fresh thyme

This is a firm favourite at Avoca. Something of a classic perhaps, but all the better for that.

Melt the butter over a very low heat, add the onions and cook gently for 10 minutes or until translucent. Raise the heat, add the mushrooms and season well with salt and pepper. Cook for 3 minutes or until the juices start to run, then stir in the flour. Lower the heat and cook, stirring continuously, for about 8 minutes to cook out the flour. Add the stock and milk to the mushroom mixture, whisking to avoid lumps. Heat the soup at just below simmering point for about 10 minutes, stirring occasionally. Add the thyme, check the seasoning and serve.

whisking to avoid lumps whisking to avoid lumps whisking

Summer berry and mint

300g raspberries
200g redcurrants, separated
from their stalks
100g blackcurrants,
separated from their stalks
50g caster sugar, or to taste
1 bunch mint, finely
chopped
single cream, or plain
yoghurt

Not all soups need to be savoury. This is a refreshing way to finish, something for one of those gloriously hot summer da

Combine the fruit with the sugar and 3 tablespoons water. Simmer gently for 5 minutes and set aside to cool.

Push though a sieve, mashing the fruit to extract as mu juice as possible. Transfer to 4 shallow soup bowls and refrigerate.

Just before serving scatter over the mint and add a generous swirl of cream or yoghurt.

Variations

Elderflowers make a welcome early summer addition. You need to poach the flowers with the fruit.

For flavour, you could also add some elderflower cordial.

Strawberries could be used in place of the raspberries.

Summer garden

4 streaky bacon rashers, diced
1 potato, peeled and diced
1 onion, peeled and diced
50g butter
2 carrots, peeled and diced
2 leeks, trimmed and diced
1 litre vegetable or chicken stock
?0g runner beans, trimmed and chopped
200g podded fresh peas, or frozen peas
250g baby spinach
2 tablespoons double cream

Sauté the bacon, potato and onion in the butter gently for 10 minutes. Add the carrot and leek and continue to cook for 5 minutes. Add the stock, season with salt and pepper, and bring to the boil. Simmer for 10-15 minutes or until everything is tender.

Add the runner beans and, 2 minutes later, the peas, and cook for a further 10 minutes. Cool for 10 minutes and add the spinach.

Reheat, swirling in a little cream to finish.

Sauté the bacon, potato and onion in the butter gently for 10 minutes

Alcohol

Whether it's a splash of wine or a slug, a little **alcohol** when cooking soups at home for adults can pep up a soup no end. Even a tinned tomato soup can benefit from a little **sherry**, some might even say it is essential.

In France the tradition is encapsulated in the phrase *faire le chabrol*, when a little **wine** is added to the end of the soup and then often drunk straight from the bowl.

Provided your soup is simmered for a few minutes there is unlikely to be any alcohol left. As to what you should use with what, let taste be your guide. **A white wine** with lighter, whiter soups (or **beer** perhaps) while **red wine** is more suited to darker more autumnal flavours, mushroom for example.

Maderia, **masala**, **port** and **sherry** are all good soup alcohols. You can add split chillies to a bottle, fill with **sherry** and add to soups for a winter kick. Be warned, the chilli strength increases over time.

Olive oil

Both simple and complex at the same time. **Olive oil** swirled into soup at the end brings a peppery complexity and an attractive finish in the form of a golden whirl or zigzag.

Olive oil can also be **flavoured or infused**; with garlic is common, but **spices** and **herbs** work well too as does **lemon**.

Try particularly with vegetable soups and with ones using pulses.

Chickepea based soups are particularly good with a swirl of olive oil, as are soups involving lentils.

Cream

Cream needs to be added after the soup is removed from the heat. Otherwise it splits and you lose the smooth silkiness which is what makes it so appealing.

Whipping cream not only reduces the amount o cream used, but when combined with herbs adds novel and interesting textu **A sort of floating cloud**.

Soured cream too, can be a welcome addition. Some prefer **crème fraich** Soured cream is traditional with borscht, but is equally good on root vegetable soups.

You can also flavour cream for added interest. **Saffron** for example, or **herbs**. How many or whic herbs is entirely up to you.

…ere are occasions when
…u want your soup to
…liver a bigger eat.
…mbers may swell, your
…up might be very rich, or
…nply lacking body. These
…e the occasions when
…hole grains are called for.

The two best options in
…ese circumstances are
…rley and **rice**. The former
…oo often overlooked - is
…oulous with lamb and very
…sy to handle.

Rice may not be quite as
…ditional, but it too is very
…eful and equally delicious.

Pasta & noodles

Pasta and **noodles**, or
noodles and **pasta**. The
arguments for which came
first can and probably will
go on for ever. Suffice to say
that both are useful for
adding to lighter soups to
provide body and weight.

In all instances it is
generally better to cook the
pasta first in salted boiling
water, refresh in cold water
and then add to the soup to
heat through.

Leaves

Green leaves add texture,
colour and body to soups.

Think of **spinach** or
sorrel, **winter greens** or
cabbage, **lettuce** or
watercress.

In many instances **leaves**
– particularly the more
fibrous ones like **spinach**
and **kale** – benefit from
blanching first in salted
boiling water and refreshing
in cold water. Indeed for
some like **kale** it really is
necessary.

Large leaves and soup
spoons don't really mix. So
roughly chop anything huge
before proceeding.

Tuscan bean

1 onion, peeled and chopped
2 tablespoons olive oil
3 celery sticks, finely diced
2 large carrots, finely diced
75g streaky bacon, cut into
bite-sized pieces
3 garlic cloves, peeled
and crushed
1 litre vegetable stock
3 x 400g cans of
chopped tomatoes
1 bay leaf
A pinch of sugar
400g canned cannellini
beans, drained and
well rinsed
1 teaspoon oregano

Sauté the onion in the olive oil for 10 minutes or until translucent. Add the celery, carrots and bacon and cook for 5 minutes. Add the garlic and cook for 1 minute, then stir i the stock and tomatoes. Season well, adding the bay leaf a sugar. Bring to the boil, then reduce the heat and simmer f 15–20 minutes, until the vegetables are cooked but still al dente. Stir in the beans and oregano and cook for 5 minute Remove the bay leaf and serve with croutons (see page 57, with some pesto on top perhaps.

Serve
with
croutons
with
some
pesto
on
top
perhaps

Seafood chowder

400g mussels
250ml milk
250ml double cream
large waxy potatoes peeled
and cut into 1cm dice
2 onions, peeled and finely
chopped
2 sticks celery, trimmed and
finely chopped
100g bacon, finely diced
50g butter
1 tablespoon plain flour
pinch cayenne pepper
400g raw prawns
200g firm white fish, like
monkfish, John Dory or sole,
cut into bite-sized pieces

An Irish take on a classic New England dish. There they stick to clams, but our mussles are too good to ignore and add a splash of striking colour to this generally white soup.

Wash the mussels thoroughly and place in a large saucepan over a high heat with the lid on. Steam for 5 to 8 minutes or until the shellfish have just opened. If you cook them for too long they will shrink and dry up. Remove from the heat and as soon as they are cool enough to handle, remove the empty half shell from each one and discard. Strain and reserve the liquid.

Heat the milk and cream together and poach the potatoes until just tender, about 8 minutes, remove from the milk and cream mixture and set aside.

Cook the onions, celery and bacon in the butter for 10-15 minutes without colouring. Stir in the flour and cayenne pepper and continue cooking for a further 2 minutes, without colouring. Pour in the strained liquid from the mussels along with the cream and milk. Return the potatoes, add the prawns and white fish and poach for 5 minutes, or until cooked. Return the mussels, heat through and check seasoning.

Most mussels sold in the shops are now grown on ropes and come fairly free of both beards and barnacles. If you are picking your own off the foreshore, ask for local advice on the best place in order to ensure quality and safety. Barnacles tend to come by the bucket-load with these self harvested specimens, but then you also get the added treat of free food. Mussels are traditionally not eaten during warmer "r in the month" months, but farming and refrigeration has generally negated this rule.

Seafood soup with Parmesan toast

Serves 6

olive oil
1 onion, peeled and finely chopped
2 garlic cloves, peeled and finely chopped
1 teaspoon fennel seeds
2 star anise
1 glass dry vermouth (125ml)
1 x 400g can tomatoes
litres light fish or chicken stock
300g mussels
150g clams
150g prawns
200g hake or gurnard
½ French stick
2 tablespoons freshly grated Parmesan

Heat 3 tablespoons of the oil and sauté the onion without colouring for 20 minutes over a low heat. Add the garlic, fennel seeds and star anise and continue cooking for 1 minute. Add the vermouth and boil off for 2 minutes.

Add the tomatoes and stock and bring to the boil, then lower the heat and simmer for 10 minutes. Slide in the clams and mussels and, 5 minutes later, the prawns and hake or gurnard. Continue cooking for 5-6 minutes or until all the fish is cooked.

Cut the bread into thin slices, drizzle with olive oil and grill until golden brown on both sides. This doesn't take long, so keep an eye out. Sprinkle over the Parmesan and serve on top or to the side of the soup.

Rouille

25g breadcrumbs
2 garlic cloves, peeled and finely chopped
1 egg yolk
2 teaspoons harissa
250ml olive oil

The traditional garnish served with fish soups in the south of France. Croûtons and grated Gruyère turn the whole event into something of a feast.

Soak the breadcrumbs in water, squeeze well, then combine with the garlic, egg yolk and harissa. Pour in a steady stream of olive oil, mixing all the time as you would for mayonnaise.

Spinach and nutmeg

50g butter
1 onion, peeled and finely chopped
2 sticks celery, chopped
2 potatoes, peeled and chopped
1 litre vegetable stock
250g spinach
1 bunch parsley, picked and chopped
¼ nutmeg, grated
4 teaspoons crème fraiche

Heat the butter over a low heat and gently soften the onio and celery for 10 minutes. Add the potato and continue to cook for a further 5 minutes.

Add the stock, bring to the boil and simmer for 10 minutes or until the potatoes are tender.

Add the spinach and parsley and cook for 5 minutes, until the spinach has just wilted. Add the nutmeg and sea: with salt and pepper. Puree in a liquidiser, check seasonir and serve with a teaspoon of crème fraiche.

If you want this soup to be really smooth and silky pa through a sieve after you have liquidised it.

to

be really

smooth and

silky

pass

through

a

sieve

Cream of smoked haddock

2 onions peeled and finely chopped
4 potatoes, peeled and finely chopped
400g smoked haddock, cut into cubes
1 litre fish or vegetable stock
200ml full-fat milk
1 tablespoon finely chopped parsley

The simplicity of this soup belies the complex flavour of naturally smoked haddock. Simplicity at its best.

Combine the onion, potatoes and fish in a saucepan with the stock. Bring slowly to the boil and simmer for 5 minutes or until the fish and potatoes are tender.

Puree in a liquidiser and return to the saucepan. Add the milk, season with salt and pepper and reheat. Scatter in the parsley and serve.

parsley

Sweet potato and lentil

25g butter
2 tablespoons olive oil
2 onions, peeled and chopped
1 medium sweet potato, peeled and chopped
1 medium carrot, roughly chopped
2 celery stalks, trimmed and chopped
150g Puy lentils
1/2 teaspoon turmeric
1 teaspoon ground cumin
a pinch of ground cinnamon
3cm piece fresh root ginger, peeled and finely chopped
3 garlic cloves, peeled and chopped
1/2 x 400g can tomatoes
1 litre chicken stock
juice of 1 lemon

Combine the butter and oil over a medium heat, add the onion and sauté for 10 minutes without colouring. Add the sweet potato, carrot, celery and lentils and coat in the oil. Add the turmeric, cumin, cinnamon, ginger and garlic, toss so they are well coated and cook for 2-3 minutes, stirring occasionally. Add the tomatoes and stock, and season with lemon juice and salt and pepper to taste. Cook for 30 minutes or until the lentils are soft and the sweet potato is tender.

Purée briefly, so everything is chunky rather than smooth. Check the seasoning, reheat and serve.

Variation
You can use brown lentils in this soup too. We frequently swap. The texture and flavours are surprisingly different

1 teaspoon black mustard seeds
juice and zest of 1 lime
4 tomatoes, deseeded and diced
1 avocado, diced
extra virgin olive oil

Fresh tomato relish

Combine the mustard seeds with the lime and set aside for 10 minutes. Combine the tomatoes and avocado with the mustard seeds and enough olive oil to bind and season with salt and pepper.

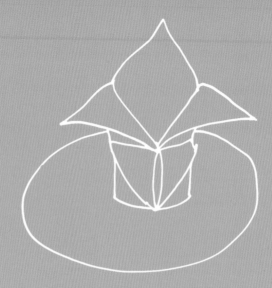

Napkin Folding

Crown

1. Take two corners of a napkin and join so you have a triangle.

2. Take the right and left corners and fold to meet the top of the triangle to form a square. Turn so you have a diamond (first drawing).

3. Take the bottom corner and bring ⅔ of the way to the top (drawing two). Then fold this corner back to the bottom (drawing three.)

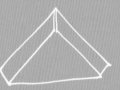

4. Turn the napkin over and tuck the far corners into each other.

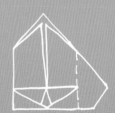

French pleat

1. Fold the napkin in four.

2. Roll the first layer into the centre.

3. Fold (do not roll) the second layer under the first.

4. Fold the next layer under the second, leaving the same width as the other two folds.

5. Fold the right and left side edges under (drawing three).

Slow-roasted plum tomato with chorizo crisps

500g plum tomatoes
1 sprig rosemary
2 garlic cloves, peeled and crushed with a little salt
olive oil
a pinch of caster sugar
8 thin slices chorizo (the salami style rather than cooking chorizo)
onion, peeled and chopped
1 red chilli, finely chopped
1 litre light chicken or vegetable stock
4 teaspoons crème fraîche
a few basil leaves

Slow-roasting may seem like something rather time consuming but once in the oven they really do look after themselves. The slow approach, something we are rather keen on at Avoca, intensifies the flavour, like homemade sun-dried but without the kick.

Preheat the oven to 110°C/gas mark ¼

Halve the tomatoes and arrange on a baking tray. Slip in the rosemary and garlic and sprinkle generously with olive oil. Season with salt and pepper and a pinch of sugar and bake for 2 hours. Add the chorizo slices on a separate shallow tray for the last 30 minutes so they crisp up.

Gently sauté the onion in 2 tablespoons olive oil for 10 minutes without colouring. Add the chilli and cook for 2 more minutes. Add the tomato mixture from the oven along with the stock and bring to the boil. Season with salt and pepper and simmer for 15 minutes. Blitz, check seasoning and reheat.

Serve with a teaspoon of crème fraîche, 2 slices of chorizo and a few basil leaves per person.

Serve
with a
teaspoon
of
crème
fraîche

Potato and herb

3 onions, peeled and
chopped
5 large potatoes, peeled
and chopped
25g butter
1 litre vegetable stock
3 leeks, trimmed and
chopped
100ml double cream
2 tablespoons finely chopped
herbs (chives and parsley)

The Irish passion for potatoes is well documented. This soup treats them as a vegetable rather than simply as a starch. You need a floury potato like a rooster rather than anything waxy.

Saute the onion in the butter without colouring for 10 minutes. Add the potato and cook for a further 5 minutes. Add the stock, season with salt and pepper and bring to the boil. Lower the heat and simmer for 20 minutes or until the vegetables are soft.

Add the leeks and cook for a further 5 minutes or until the leeks are soft. Liquidise, return to the pan, stir in the cream and check the seasoning.

Serve with the chopped herbs sprinkled over the top.

Variations

Other herbs to consider include dill, tarragon, mint, rosemary (sparingly) and thyme.

Red pepper and sweetcorn

2 red peppers
3 tablespoons olive oil
1 onion, peeled and chopped
1 bay leaf
1 bunch parsley, finely chopped
1 red chilli, finely chopped
1 400g tin tomatoes
450g tinned sweetcorn

Grill or roast the red peppers until well charred. Transfer to bowl, cover with clingfilm and leave to cool. Deseed and remove the skin.

Heat the olive oil over a low heat and gently sauté the onion without colouring for 10 minutes. Add the bay leaf, parsley, chilli and tomatoes, season with salt and pepper and cook for 5 minutes. Liquidise and return to the pan. Roughly chop the peppers and add to the tomatoes. Add the sweetcorn, heat slowly, check seasoning and serve.

Red cabbage with sausages

*4 tablespoons olive oil plus
extra for the end
8 good quality large pure
pork sausages
medium onion, peeled and
finely sliced
ticks celery, finely chopped
2 carrots, diced
00g shredded red cabbage,
core and outside leaves
removed
2 garlic cloves, peeled
and chopped
2 tins chopped tomatoes
2 litres chicken stock
1 x 400g tin cannellini
beans, drained and rinsed
slices good country bread
1 garlic clove, halved*

Heat the oil and colour the sausages over a moderate heat.
Remove and set aside. Add the onion, celery and carrots to
the hot oil and saute for 10-15 minutes or until soft but not
coloured.

Add the cabbage and continue to cook, turning in the
hot oil, for 10 minutes, or until it starts to wilt. Add the
garlic, tomatoes and stock and season with salt and pepper.
Add the sausages, cover and simmer for 40 minutes.

Add the beans and continue to cook for a further 15
minutes. Toast the bread and rub with garlic.

Spoon the soup into large wide bowls, place the toasts
on top and

drizzle

over

a

good

slug

of

olive

oil

.

Stock

When you sit back because you are bowled over by the flavour of a soup what is going on? Is it the flavours, the deep rounded notes sitting in the background, the combination of ingredients, the skill of the cook? It is all of these thing but chief among them is the stock. This is the bedrock of soupmaking, responsible for the rich, full-bodied complexity that brings a wow factor. Sort the stock and you are sorted, literally. Its hard to go wrong after that.

The importance of stock is recognised world wide. In Asia it is often a light chicken stock, in France it tends to be more complex but it gives to soup that wonderful rounded background against which the other flavours are shown to best effect. Nowhere is the adage of less is more seen as clearly as in the making of dashi, the Japanese combination of fish and seaweed. A chef in Japan is measured by his ability to balance the flavours in this highly delicate broth.

Stock making need not be complicated, or indeed that time consuming. Some of the bought stock cubes are better than others.

Some better brands include Marigold and Kallo.

A few notes on stockmaking

1. A big saucepan is not essential, but helps
2. Add enough water to cover the ingredients generously. As the point of the exercise is to transfer the flavour of the ingredients into the liquid you don't want too much liquid
3. If you are using meat or bones a scum will form on top as the stock approaches boiling point. These proteins need to be scooped off to avoid the stock becoming cloudy
4. Once the stock is boiling lower the heat, you want the merest simmer
5. Do you season? A vexed question as some do and some don't. The danger of seasoning is that as the stock reduces the whole assembly becomes too salty.
Far better to leave the seasoning for when you make your soup when you can adjust things in real time.
6. How long? About four hours for meat stock, two hours for chicken and 30 minutes for fish and vegetable.

7. Once the stock is finished strain and cool. Remove an fat from the surface. This i best done by chilling the stock down in the fridge. Alternatively lay sheets of kitchen paper on the surfa the fat will adhere to the paper and then discard. Continue till you get dowr to the liquid (you'll know this because the fat starts appear as globules

Vegetables (and their trimmings) suitabl for stockmaking

Asparagus, aubergine, bea broccoli, carrots, cauliflow celery, fennel, leeks, lentil lettuce, mushrooms, nettle (!), onions, tomatoes.

A fresh stock is hard to b A good stock cube (Gallo, Marigold or Kello) can get you out of a fix
A good stock cube cooked with water and a few vegetables shows real styl
Good stock forms the bas of any good soup. In a vegetable-based soup we u a vegetable stock. This is partly to satisfy vegetarian customers. Most vegetable soups taste even better wi

ght chicken stock. Chicken
ock is by far the best all-
ounder. Making stock does
quire a little time and care.
ou can make stock in 30
inutes, but an hour, or even
vo will produce something
finitely better.

Chicken stock for when you're not in a hurry

chicken, roughly chopped
50g pork bones
onion, roughly chopped
carrots, chopped
leeks, sliced
stick celery, chopped

it the chicken and pork
ones in a large pan, cover
ith cold water and bring
most to the boil. Turn the
eat right down and simmer
r 30 minutes, skimming off
ly froth that rises to the
rface.
dd the vegetables and
lough water to cover, bring
most to the boil again,
wer the heat and simmer
r a further 30 minutes.
emove from the
eat and allow to cool.
rain off the liquid, return
the saucepan and simmer
r an hour, uncovered.

Chicken stock for when you are in a hurry

1 good-quality chicken stock
cube
250g uncooked chicken
thighs or wings
1 leek, finely chopped
1 carrot, finely chopped

Combine everything in a pan,
add the water and bring
almost to boiling point, lower
the heat and simmer for 30
minutes. Strain and proceed.

Chicken stock instantly

1 good-quality chicken stock
cube
1 leek, finely chopped
1 carrot, roughly chopped
1 stick celery, chopped

Combine all the ingredients
in a pan, cover with the
water, bring to the boil,
strain and proceed.

Vegetable stock when you're not in a hurry

200g potatoes, washed and
chopped
1 butternut squash, peeled,
deseeded and chopped
2 carrots, chopped
2 tablespoons chopped
tinned tomatoes

1 onions, chopped
1 leek, chopped
3 sticks celery, chopped

Roughly chop all the
vegetables and put in a large
pan with enough water to
cover. Bring to the boil, then
lower the heat to a gentle
simmer and cook,
uncovered, for two hours.
Turn off the heat, allow to
cool and strain.
Season with salt and sugar
to taste

Vegetable stock when you are in a hurry

a good-quality vegetable
stock cube
2 carrots, roughly chopped
few sprigs of flat-leaf parsley

Place all the ingredients in a
large pan, cover with water
and bring to the boil, lower
the heat and simmer for
10–15 minutes if time, then
strain.

Editor Hugo Arnold
Photography Georgia Glynn Smith
Art Direction and Design Lucy Gowans
Production Tim Chester

First published in 2007 by Avoca Ltd,
Kilmacanogue, Co Wicklow
Reprinted in 2008 (twice), 2009 (three times), 2010

Printed and bound in Hong Kong by Great Wall
Printing Company

Cataloguing-in-publication datea:
A catalogue record for this book is available
from the British Library
ISBN 978-0-9538152-2-7